THE HEART OF THE JUNGLE

THIS BOOK BELONGS TO

_____

FOR THE KIDS WHO WANT TO EXPLORE

ISBN: 9798894583129

DEEP IN THE HEART OF THE GREENLEAF JUNGLE,
,A YOUNG LION CUB NAMED ZUZU LIVED WITH HIS FAMILY AND
FRIENDS. THE JUNGLE WAS FULL OF LIFE, COLOR, AND ADVENTURE.

ZUZU LOVED CHASING BUTTERFLIES, LISTENING TO THE BIRDS SING AND
SPLASHING IN THE COOL RIVER. THE JUNGLE WAS HIS HOME, AND HE FELT
SAFE AND HAPPY.

ONE MORNING, ZUZU WOKE UP TO A STRANGE, LOUD NOISE.
"RUMBLE! CRASH!" THE GROUND SHOOK BENEATH HIS PAWS.
"WHAT IS THAT?" HE WONDERED.

CURIOUS, ZUZU FOLLOWED THE SOUND THROUGH THE TREES. WHEN HE REACHED A CLEARING, HIS EYES WIDENED IN SHOCK. GIANT MACHINES WERE KNOCKING DOWN TREES!

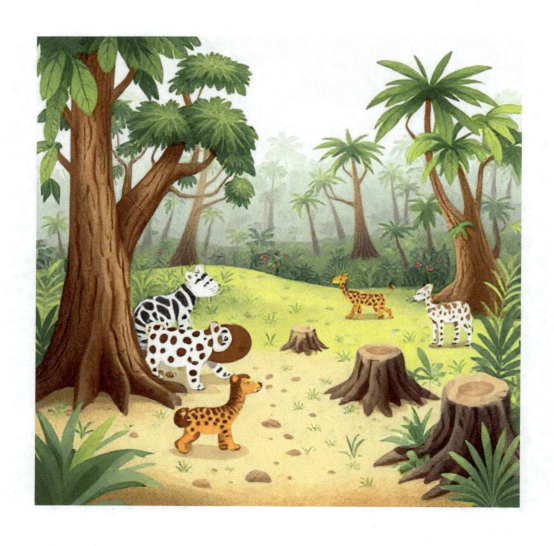

HUMANS WERE CUTTING THE JUNGLE, AND ANIMALS WERE RUNNING IN FEAR. THE ONCE-GREEN LAND WAS TURNING INTO STUMPS AND DUST. ZUZU'S HEART POUNDED.

HE RAN BACK TO HIS FRIENDS—TIKO THE MONKEY, BELLA THE PARROT, AND ZANE THE ZEBRA. "THE JUNGLE IS IN DANGER! WE HAVE TO STOP THEM!" ZUZU CRIED.

"BUT HOW?" TIKO ASKED. "THEY'RE SO BIG, AND THEIR MACHINES ARE STRONG!"
BELLA FLAPPED HER WINGS. "WE NEED A CLEVER PLAN!"

ZUZU THOUGHT HARD. "IF THE HUMANS SEE HOW SPECIAL OUR JUNGLE IS, MAYBE THEY WILL STOP!" HIS FRIENDS NODDED. IT WAS WORTH A TRY!

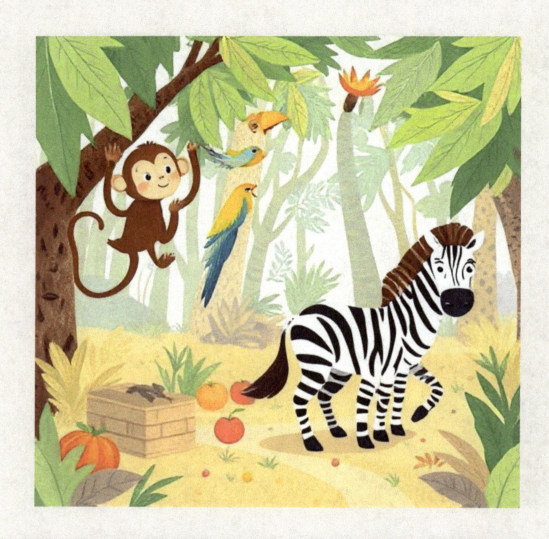

THE ANIMALS GOT TO WORK. TIKO GATHERED THE BRIGHTEST FRUITS. BELLA CALLED BIRDS TO SING. ZANE AND THE ZEBRAS MADE PATHS THROUGH THE JUNGLE.

ZUZU RAN TO FIND MORE ANIMALS. "COME HELP US!" HE
ROARED. ELEPHANTS, DEER, AND EVEN TINY ANTS JOINED IN.
EVERYONE HAD A JOB TO DO.

THE NEXT MORNING, WHEN THE LOGGERS RETURNED, THEY STOPPED IN SURPRISE.
THE JUNGLE WAS BURSTING WITH COLOR, MUSIC, AND LIFE!

BIRDS CHIRPED IN HARMONY, BUTTERFLIES DANCED, AND
FIREFLIES TWINKLED LIKE STARS. MONKEYS SWUNG THROUGH
TREES, TOSSING FRUITS LIKE A WELCOME FEAST.

ONE WORKER LOOKED AROUND. "WOW! THIS PLACE IS BEAUTIFUL! MAYBE WE SHOULDN'T CUT IT DOWN," HE SAID, LOWERING HIS AXE.

A SCIENTIST WITH THE GROUP TOOK OUT A NOTEBOOK. "THIS JUNGLE IS HOME TO RARE ANIMALS! DESTROYING IT WOULD BE A HUGE MISTAKE."

ZUZU BRAVELY STEPPED FORWARD AND LET OUT A MIGHTY ROAR. THE HUMANS STARED. "EVEN THE LION IS PROTECTING HIS HOME," ONE WHISPERED.

THE HEAD WORKER SCRATCHED HIS CHIN. "MAYBE WE SHOULD STOP AND THINK. THIS JUNGLE IS TOO SPECIAL TO DESTROY."

THE TEAM MADE A CALL. SOON, MORE PEOPLE ARRIVED—SCIENTISTS, REPORTERS, AND GOVERNMENT OFFICIALS. THEY TOOK PICTURES AND NOTES.

"THE WORLD MUST KNOW ABOUT THIS PLACE!" A REPORTER SAID.
"IF WE SHARE THIS JUNGLE'S STORY, PEOPLE WILL WANT TO PROTECT IT !"

A FEW DAYS LATER, A LARGE SIGN WAS PLACED AT THE JUNGLE'S ENTRANCE: "PROTECTED WILDLIFE AREA - NO CUTTING ALLOWED!"

ZUZU AND HIS FRIENDS CHEERED. THE LOGGERS LEFT, AND IN THEIR PLACE, VISITORS CAME TO ADMIRE NATURE INSTEAD OF DESTROYING IT.

TIKO SWUNG FROM THE TREES. "WE DID IT, ZUZU!" BELLA FLAPPED HER WINGS. "OUR HOME IS SAFE FOREVER!" ZANE STOMPED JOYFULLY.

ZUZU SMILED.

"WE PROVED THAT EVERY CREATURE, BIG OR SMALL, CAN MAKE A DIFFERENCE."

SOON, THE JUNGLE BECAME A PLACE WHERE CHILDREN, SCIENTISTS, AND TRAVELERS CAME TO LEARN ABOUT NATURE AND WILDLIFE.

PEOPLE PLANTED NEW TREES, HELPED ANIMALS, AND PROMISED TO
KEEP THE JUNGLE SAFE. ZUZU FELT PROUD.

ONE DAY, A YOUNG CHILD VISITING THE JUNGLE ASKED, "WHO SAVED THIS PLACE?" A GUIDE SMILED AND POINTED.

"THAT YOUNG LION OVER THERE," THE GUIDE SAID. "ZUZU, THE LION WHO SAVED HIS JUNGLE!"

ZUZU'S HEART SWELLED WITH PRIDE. HE KNEW HIS HOME WOULD BE SAFE FOR MANY YEARS TO COME.

UNDER THE GOLDEN SUNSET, HE SAT ON A HIGH ROCK, WATCHING OVER HIS BEAUTIFUL, GREEN WORLD.

HIS ROAR ECHOED THROUGH THE JUNGLE,
A SOUND OF VICTORY, STRENGTH, AND HOPE.

THE JUNGLE WAS ALIVE, AND THANKS TO ZUZU, IT WOULD STAY THAT WAY FOREVER.

ANIMALS PLAYED FREELY, BIRDS SANG, AND TREES STOOD TALL, SWAYING GENTLY IN THE WIND.

ZUZU LEARNED THAT ONE SMALL IDEA, WITH TEAMWORK AND COURAGE, COULD CHANGE THE WORLD.

HIS STORY SPREAD FAR AND WIDE, INSPIRING CHILDREN AND ANIMALS EVERYWHERE TO PROTECT NATURE.

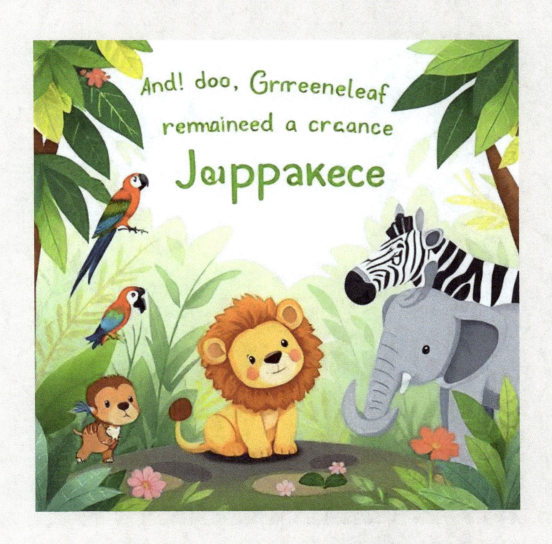

AND SO, GREENLEAF JUNGLE REMAINED A PARADISE, WHERE CREATURES
BIG AND SMALL LIVED IN PEACE.

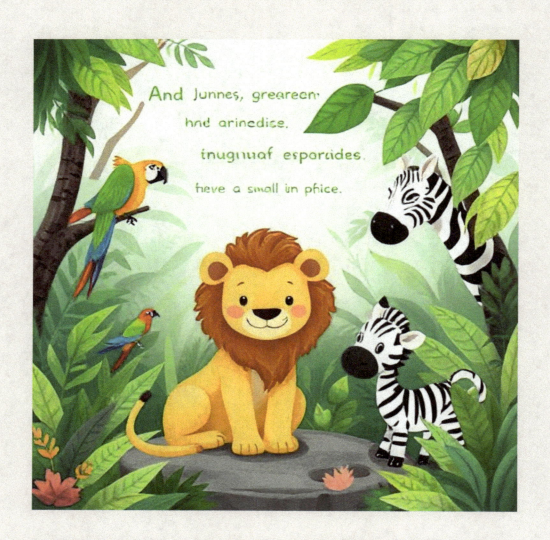

ZUZU KNEW HE WAS JUST A CUB, BUT IN HIS HEART, HE HAD BECOME THE JUNGLE'S TRUE KING.